His Power In My Words

Karen L. Northern

ROYSTON
Publishing

BK Royston Publishing
P. O. Box 4321
Jeffersonville, IN 47131
502-802-5385
http://www.bkroystonpublishing.com
bkroystonpublishing@gmail.com

© Copyright – 2017

All Rights Reserved. No part of this book may be reproduced, stored in a retrieval system, or transmitted by any means without the written permission of the author.

Cover Design: Bill Lacy
Photo Credit for Back Cover: Kyler S. Northern
Photo Makeup: Aliya Granger
Photo Hair: Shannon Shorts
Photoshoot Style Consultant: Meoshuh Jackson

ISBN-10: 1-946111-18-X
ISBN-13: 978-1-946111-18-0

Printed in the United States of America

DEDICATION

This book is dedicated to my late parents Lawrence Northern, Sr. and Roberta R. Northern. Thank you for always encouraging me to dream and in doing so; turning those dreams into realities.

TABLE OF CONTENTS

Foreword

My Poems	1
My Prayers	15
My Devotions	33

Foreword

I thank and praise God for the His power, strength, and peace to quiet every voice so I could begin to hear what He would say to me:

"I will stand upon my watch, and set me upon the tower, and will watch to see what he will say unto me, and what I shall answer when I am reproved.

² And the Lord answered me, and said, write the vision, and make it plain upon tables, that he may run that readeth it.

³ For the vision is yet for an appointed time, but at the end it shall speak, and not lie: though it tarry, wait for it; because it will surely come, it will not tarry."- Habakkuk 2:1-3

But the people that do know their God shall be strong and do exploits. Daniel 11:32b

I was prompted to write again and not allow my thoughts to lie dormant in my mind, the Lord came quickly to persuade me through His Spirit, His people, and His Word to propel me into my next door. This was a door I previously closed through disobedience and allowed the busyness of life to be the reason for not opening it again. I had always been told that I could "turn a phrase" or that I had a "quick mind," but I know I walk through this open door only through His grace and mercy.

His Spirit gave my mere words life to speak to others and ignite the fire in my soul. Every bit of doubt preventing my spirit from being shifted from its rightful and primary place was burned away. I am eternally grateful for the voice of God and His sanctifying sound that pierced through the clutter in my mind to give me the nudge I needed to express His power in my words!

I pray that You hear His still, small voice in every line because I can never, ever take credit for HIS POWER in my words!

HIS POWER
IN My Words

His Power My Words

My Poems

REVIVED

You created within me a clean heart,

Knew that I needed to be set apart.

From those who would try to lead me astray,

To what Your Blood and Glory had won on that Great Day.

On that day You died for me and bought me for such a high price,

I thought I was such a roll of the dice.

But You made me to realize I was not the booby prize,

You called me the apple of Your eye and I won't be denied the victory of Your gift ETERNAL

LIFE: I AM REVIVED!

Karen L. Northern

THE CALLED

As I make my way to the side of the bed,

Wondering where I am, not knowing my feet from my head

It is amazingly apparent that it is a new day and new mercies I see.

A new day lies ahead full of benefits, Godly purpose, and destiny.

It is only because Your goodness and compassion faileth not,

Faithful is the God I serve, so I lift up my hands in praise with all I've got!

It doesn't take long for me to realize that Jesus, Lord of lords, the Alpha and Omega,

The Beginning and the End, my All and All,

He has given me yet another chance, another start, pushed reset, rewind;

Yes, I am the called!

WHEN YOUR SON IS THE KING
(My Cross To Bear – Seen Through Mary's Eyes)

As I look back over my life, I never expected to be given the blessed privilege to bear

THE King.

I was young, poor, betrothed and with child by the Holy Spirit;

I could hardly negotiate in my mind such a thing.

I surely thought I would be left on my own to bear the shame of single parenthood,

The angel Gabriel who visited me to announce I would conceive left me ill at ease; yet I knew it would all work out for my good.

Now the courage I gained to walk this thing out came from within,

Jesus, the Messiah, Yeshua, Immanuel, Holy One of Israel resided not only in my womb but also in my inner being.

At His birth the heavenly host, shepherds, magi and wise men declared His majesty both near and far,

I began to realize that He NEVER belonged to me, I was His vessel to be used, and he was no longer just my son but now my Savior.

As He grew apart from me and more knowledgeable in the things concerning our Father in heaven whom we both loved and adored,

The cross that I would bear appeared in my mind's eye and there it was permanently stored.

Karen L. Northern

As He left our home to choose those who would walk with Him in the work that was required to save many lives,

I felt deserted, left behind, kicked to the curb, forgotten even dead inside.

Those He chose forgot Him in His greatest time of need, but He forged ahead and I followed Him to Calvary for a sight that I will have forever etched in my brain,

My weeping turned to joy three days later when He rose with POWER.

Now the One who I was privileged to birth, nurse, love, and serve is

NOW ALIVE FOREVER.

REST IN HIM

As I lie here not quite able to move on my own body,

I lift my hands to the heavens to the One, and I am assured that I am His alone.

I realize the rest I desire is not gained from a positional place such as prone, side lying or supine;

I must press into my Prince of Peace, my Savior in whom I will find rest divine,

In His rest, there is peace, salvation, contentment, healing, deliverance, and joy.

Jesus, my Redeemer, whose rest, and mind I receive now and forevermore.

Karen L. Northern

THE TRUTH

We hold these truths to be self-evident...

See, I almost had you; believing in speeches, declarations that only mere men can speak or invent.

Here are a few truths that are one to grow on:

We will go back further than 1776 to over 2000 years ago to which the TRUTH is built upon.

God's intentional, intelligent purpose was to create a creature who would glorify ONLY Him;

Somewhere, somehow we got it mixed up, twisted, boasting in I, me, we, and them.

So, to sum it up; this is the only truth that I can truthfully hold to be truly self-evident;

We know for sure our Lord and Savior paid and bought us with such a high price and preciousness.

AN AUTUMN'S NIGHT DREAM PRAYER

As crispness is now on every passing breeze,

I pray refreshing from the Lord fulfill my needs with ease.

As I look to the hills which will soon be sun-capped and white,

I continually walk by faith and never by sight.

I know of the Lord's love both true and everlasting.

I feel it even more by His Spirit with much prayer and fasting.

I know the Lord has answered my Autumn's Night Dream and every prayer sent.

I praise and thank Him more for lost souls, weary, burdened, heavy and spent.

As the gospel of His great Word comes to my ears and heart through my Autumn's Night Dream or Spirit-sent vision,

It commits my life to our Soon-Coming King; our Savior in full and total surrender is my only wise decision.

Karen L. Northern

BELIEVE TO SEE

When the day breaks, the sun is high in the sky or even when dusk quiets the evening sky,

I look to the Father in prayer not tangibly but in my mind's eye.

The enemy comes to create a battlefield in my mind and attempts to wage war, cast imaginations, and consistently looks for a fight,

However, he is met every time with weapons of my warfare, with the full armor of God and he is sent to flight.

My mind is the place he thinks he can run free-range because he knows the people, places and things I have known.

The blessing comes to fruition when knowing of my God, and I have this intimacy about my real destination, which is what my mind was shown.

I am continually set at ease, a freedom, a peace, and emancipation that no tangibles can replicate or truly ever be.

I would have grown weary, given up and shut down, if the Immutable, Intangibility of my God I had not believed I would see.

YOU ARE MY DAUGHTER

(To A Daughter Given By God)

Although you were never formed inside my womb;

I pray that you know the love I have for you is pure and you never have to assume.

I was not present when you took your first steps, lost your teeth, wore pigtails or for other milestones.

God positioned me to watch you blossom and has blessed you to be both chronologically and physically grown.

_____, you are my daughter in every possible way that matters most.

I am in awe of how our God strategically planted you into my life so for this blessed gift in His name alone do I boast.

Karen L. Northern

SETTLED

Just because every little thing doesn't seem to go my way;

It does not mean my God loves me any less today.

Yes, I have suffered, been through, and walked the "wilderness trail" like many others.

Through it all, my Savior Jesus has stayed close and loved me closer than any brother.

As I press into Him, I become astutely aware of every trial and test and I realized each was "tailor-made" for me; I am well suited.

I am settled, planted, stablished in my Savior Jesus; forever like a tree planted am I deeply and firmly rooted.

COUNSELOR

He speaks softly but swift,

Especially when the heart and mind are painfully adrift.

As I look into the mirror not always liking what I see;

He deftly and lovingly reminds me every truth He has spoken about me.

With every objection, sustainment, overruling accusation the enemy can dish out,

He leads me and guides me into all truth away from all fear, mistrust and doubt.

Wonderful Counselor, Everlasting Father, Altogether Lovely, Mighty in Power;

Holy Spirit, Truth-Teller, my Inward Witness it is in You I run and am safe. You are my Strong tower.

HE REMEMBERS ME

Just when I thought He forgot about me,

A new anointing and refreshing made by His Spirit I did see.

The more I give in service to Him; the Holy Spirit opens my heart, my mind, and my ears to hear His voice;

To drown out fear and doubt I allowed it to live there rent-free by choice.

You see, it is as simple as binding my mind to the Mind of One who rules Supreme,

Christ Jesus, Messiah, the Anointing, the Anointed from who all see, hope, live, move and have their being and dream.

My Prayers

His Power My Words

Lord of Hosts,

We thank You for Your touch this morning. You have knowledge of what we are in need of before we ask or think it! You are the Almighty God, Omniscient, Omnipresent and You are El Eleyon, the most High God! There is nothing too hard for you!

We thank You for Your touch today that is bringing healing and wholeness to those in need of Your touch, renewed grace, and a fresh anointing!

We thank you Lord God that Your healing and grace have smiled down on us today as Your people. Thank you Father God that You are merciful and mindful to visit us and that You hear from heaven regarding our petitions for healing for every daughter, son, mother, and father. For all of our seniors who experience health challenges, those who are homebound, Father God please restore, rejuvenate, lift bowed-down heads, and rekindle that which was extinguished in the flood sent by the enemy. THANK YOU FOR LIFTING UP A YOUR STANDARD AGAINST THESE THINGS IN THE MIGHTY NAME OF JESUS!

Guide us by Your eye, O Lord! Order our steps! Lord, for every marriage, job, home, child, school system, our nation, President, neighborhoods, and foreign countries, breathe winds of change on us! We are your people, your handiwork! Glory to Your name! We pray and glorify Your name: ...we have this treasure in earthen vessels, that the excellence of the power may be of God and not of us. We are hard-pressed on every side, yet not crushed; we are perplexed, but not in despair; persecuted, but not forsaken; struck down, but not destroyed— always carrying about in the body the dying of the Lord Jesus, that the life of Jesus also may be manifested in our body. For we who live are always delivered to death for Jesus' sake, that the life of Jesus also may be manifested in our mortal flesh. So then, death is working in us, but life in you. For our light affliction, which is but for a moment, is working for us a far more exceeding and eternal weight of glory, (II Corinthians 4:7-12, 17 NKJV).

Let us reason together that we might examine ourselves and empty out old ways so Your newness might enter so that You are glorified in it! In Jesus' name, Amen!

Karen L. Northern

Gracious Father,

We enter Your gates with thanksgiving and into Your courts with praise!

Elohim, we thank You that it was Your intelligent, intentional purpose to create us in Your image. In doing so, Lord God, we have dominion over all in this earth as we are seated in heavenly places with You and all things are under our feet! We honor that seat by being good stewards over all You have given us! We plead the precious blood of Jesus over all You have given us to be accountable for and don't take it lightly! We glory in the knowledge that we are loaded with godly benefits and are humbled in the majesty of Your purpose for us! We were never created to chase after worldly possessions, because You know EXACTLY what we have need of, Father God! You chose us before the foundation of this world meaning our destiny was settled in heaven before we were even born into this wicked world! HALLELUJAH! GLORY TO Your NAME, JESUS FOR PREDESTINATION!

We pray, not only for lifting up Your name for the salvation which we possess, but also thanking You for those still lost and don't know who they are in You: Not that I have already attained, or am already perfected; but I press on, that I may lay hold of that for which Christ Jesus has also laid hold of me. Brethren, I do not count myself to have apprehended; but one thing I do, forgetting those things which are behind and reaching forward to those things which are ahead, I press toward the goal for the prize of the upward call of God in Christ Jesus. Therefore let us, as many as are mature, have this mind; and if in anything You think otherwise, God will reveal even this to you. Nevertheless, to the degree that we have already attained, let us walk by the same rule, let us be of the same mind. Brethren, join in following my example, and note those who so walk, as You have us for a pattern. For many walk, of whom I have told You often, and now tell You even weeping, that they are the enemies of the cross of Christ: whose end is destruction, whose god is their belly, and whose glory is in their shame— who set their mind on earthly things. For our citizenship is in heaven, from which we also eagerly wait for the Savior, the Lord Jesus Christ, who will transform our lowly body that it may be conformed to His glorious body, according to the working by which He is able even to subdue all things to Himself. (Philippians 3:12-21NKJV). We thank You that we are in this world but are not of it! Therefore, we are not subject to its evil because we are spirit-led! We bless You and seal this prayer in Jesus' name, Amen!!

Karen L. Northern

Lord God,

We glory in You today for who You are; abiding in Your word and thanking You for a newness of life, a clean heart and a right spirit! We thank You that Your Spirit continuously purges from us from all leaven and that we are new creatures! O, but for the blood of Jesus that has redeemed us!

Lord God, we submit to Your will and not our own selfish needs and desires. We bind our minds to the mind of Christ, renewing our thoughts, shifting our perspectives so that it lines up with Your plan and purpose for our lives!

We hear You, Lord and obey; so we pray: Knowing that a man is not justified by the works of the law, but by the faith of Jesus Christ, even we have believed in Jesus Christ, that we might be justified by the faith of Christ, and not by the works of the law: for by the works of the law shall no flesh be justified. But if, while we seek to be justified by Christ, we ourselves also are found sinners, is therefore Christ the minister of sin? God forbid. For if I build again the things which I destroyed, I make myself a transgressor. For I through the law am dead to the law, that I might live unto God. I am crucified with Christ: nevertheless I live; yet not I, but Christ liveth in me: and the life which I now live in the flesh I live by the faith of the Son of God, who loved me, and gave himself for me. I do not frustrate the grace of God: for if righteousness come by the law, then Christ is dead in vain. (Galatians 2:16-21 KJV).

We give You glory that we are spirit-filled, hidden in Christ, dead to this world, of the household of the Lord, seated in heavenly places with all things under our feet; all because You counted us worthy! We bless You and pray these and all things in Jesus' name, Amen!

His Power My Words

Father God,

We thank You this evening for true worship and the provision of the Holy Spirit who teaches us to rightly divide Your word! We thank You that we are continually kept as light in a dark world that You might be glorified! Lord, thank You for keeping us in all our ways. We pray for ourselves and intercede for our brothers and sisters: For you were once darkness, but now you are light in the Lord. Walk as children of light (for the fruit of the Spirit is in all goodness, righteousness, and truth), finding out what is acceptable to the Lord, in addition, do not have fellowship with the unfruitful works of darkness. Instead, expose them for it is shameful even to speak of those things that are done by them in secret. However, all things that are exposed are made manifest by the light, for whatever makes manifest is light. Therefore, He says, "Awake, you who sleep, Arise from the dead, And Christ will give you light." See then that you walk circumspectly, not as fools but as wise, redeeming the time, because the days are evil. Therefore, do not be unwise, but understand what the will of the Lord is. (Ephesians 5:8-17 NKJV). We proclaim the acceptable year of the Lord because Your spirit lives in us! We pray that Your house, _____ continues to be sanctified for Your use, operates in excellence unto honor for Your will and good pleasure, O Lord God! Bless our Pastor who works diligently to serve You, labor for us and lead as You guide him/ her! Cover him/her with Your wings that none can harm him/her. We thank You that our Pastor is always subject to Your Spirit; so the right information comes at the right time and in the right places. We thank You that our Pastor receives uninterrupted rest and is refreshed for every day's work. We consecrate and roll our works unto You, rejoicing evermore, praying without ceasing because we know this is Your will concerning us in Christ Jesus! We lift up Your name for there is none greater than You are Jesus and we pray this and all things in Your name, Amen!

Karen L. Northern

Everlasting Father,

We give thanks on today and rejoice that we are drawn nearer to You through the precious blood of Jesus! Every promise, benefit and grace is ours through His precious blood! Healing, restoration and revival is in the blood is Jesus! We thank that the life of the flesh is in the blood! We know that we were purchased with a precious high price and we thank you. Lord God, we thank You for being the Shepherd and Bishop of our souls!

Father, we thank You that we are Your chosen and the called because of the blood! We pray and humbly submit our lives to you, knowing: for the law made nothing perfect; on the other hand, there is the bringing in of a better hope, through which we draw near to God. By so much more, Jesus has become a surety of a better covenant. Therefore, He is also able to save to the uttermost those who come to God through Him, since He always lives to make intercession for them. For such a High Priest was fitting for us, who is holy, harmless, undefiled, separate from sinners, and has become higher than the heavens; who does not need daily, as those high priests, to offer up sacrifices, first for His own sins and then for the people's, for this He did once for all when He offered up Himself. For the law appoints as high priests men who have weakness, but the word of the oath, which came after the law, appoints the Son who has been perfected forever. (Hebrews 7:19, 22, 25-28 NKJV). We are made perfect through the blood! Lord, we plead Your blood over everybody in need of healing, every heart in need in restoration, and every mind in need of renewal! Thank You, Lord for making us fellow laborers in prayer and being an intercessor for us through Your Holy Spirit! We glorify You because You are worthy, in Jesus' name, Amen!

Soon-Coming King,

We worship You in spirit and truth! We praise you, Lord God for Your testimonies are sure and are a delight to us!

We pray for comfort, peace and strength for our church but especially those who are in need of Your touch right now and in the days to come! We pray for the body of Christ at large, the nation, government officials, school systems and officials, Lord God! We thank You for giving them Godly wisdom and that instruction is pleasant to them all. We thank You that every Christian seated in leadership positions will stand in their rightful places. We thank You Father God that any in need of protection; knows You as Jehovah Nissi. We thank You thank You for healing the land and comforting those that mourn in Zion that they be comforted with a comfort wherewith they might comfort others! We pray Your peace and love which is shed abroad in our hearts through the Holy Spirit whom You gave us as a gift!

We pray rejoicing: For I determined not to know anything among you, save Jesus Christ, and him crucified. However, as it is written, Eye hath not seen, nor ear heard, neither have entered into the heart of man, the things which God hath prepared for them that love him. But God hath revealed them unto us by his Spirit: for the Spirit searcheth all things, yea, the deep things of God. For what man knoweth the things of a man, save the spirit of man that is in him? Even so, the things of God knoweth no man, but the Spirit of God. Now we have received, not the spirit of the world, but the spirit that is of God; that we might know the things that are freely given to us of God. (1 Corinthians 2:2, 9-12 KJV)! We give thanks in all things, in the mighty name of Jesus, Amen!

Karen L. Northern

Most High God,

This morning we are grateful and we look up to You who hold all things in Your hands and we do not look at our circumstances for we know they are temporal! We thank You that healing has come, wholeness has come, and a newness of life is ours! A fresh anointing is here! New mercies are ours because You are faithful! O GLORY TO YOUR NAME, LORD OF HOSTS!!

We magnify You, believe You alone and pray: Who has believed our report? And to whom has the arm of the Lord been revealed? For He shall grow up before Him as a tender plant, And as a root out of dry ground. He has no form or comeliness; and when we see Him, there is no beauty that we should desire Him. He is despised and rejected by men, A Man of sorrows and acquainted with grief. And we hid, as it were, our faces from Him; He was despised, and we did not esteem Him. Surely, He has borne our griefs and carried our sorrows; yet we esteemed Him stricken, Smitten by God, and afflicted. But He was wounded for our transgressions, He was bruised for our iniquities; the chastisement for our peace was upon Him, and by His stripes, we are healed. All we like sheep have gone astray; we have turned, every one, to his own way; and the Lord has laid on Him the iniquity of us all. He was oppressed and He was afflicted, Yet He opened not His mouth; He was led as a lamb to the slaughter, and as a sheep before its shearers is silent, So He opened not His mouth. He was taken from prison and from judgment, and who will declare His generation? For He was cut off from the land of the living; for the transgressions of my people He was stricken. And they made His grave with the wicked— but with the rich at His death, Because He had done no violence, Nor was any deceit in His mouth. Yet it pleased the Lord to bruise Him; He has put Him to grief. When You make His soul an offering for sin, He shall see His seed, He shall prolong His days, And the pleasure of the Lord shall prosper in His hand. He shall see the labor of His soul, and be satisfied. By His knowledge, My righteous Servant shall justify many, for He shall bear their iniquities. Therefore, I will divide Him a portion with the great, and He shall divide the spoil with the strong, Because He poured out His soul unto death, And He was numbered with the transgressors, and He bore the sin of many, And made intercession for the transgressors. (Isaiah 53:1-12 NKJV). The blood of Jesus is against every operating spirit of satan! There is none like you, Jesus! We plead Your precious blood over our minds, emotions, bodies that are the temples of the Holy Spirit and our will, which we submit unto you! We pray all in Jesus' name, Amen!

Karen L. Northern

Father God,

With all my heart, mind, and body, I give You praise! You have sustained us through times that even in our own finite minds; we have still to comprehend Your greatness! O Lord God, You are past finding out! Lord, consume this praise that Your glory shall prevail! Wondrous and marvelous are thy works unto Your people, Lord! We cannot praise and worship You enough to show our appreciation but here, O Lord, we sacrifice a praise unto You today! We give thanks in ALL things!

We serve every enemy notice on today that Your anointing is upon us and we receive it with hearts and minds toward you! We plead the blood of Jesus against every and any operation that would cause us to faint in our minds, spirits or faith concerning You and Your will! O Lord, we are fully persuaded that we as a body at Rehoboth are as the Word says: For I say, through the grace given unto me, to every man that is among you, not to think of himself more highly than he ought to think; but to think soberly, according as God hath dealt to every man the measure of faith. For as we have many members in one body, and all members have not the same office: So we, being many, are one body in Christ, and every one members one of another. Having then gifts differing according to the grace that is given to us, whether prophecy, let us prophesy according to the proportion of faith; Or ministry, let us wait on our ministering: or he that teaches, on teaching; Or he that exhorted, on exhortation: he that giveth, let him do it with simplicity; he that ruleth, with diligence; he that sheweth mercy, with cheerfulness. Let love be without dissimulation. Abhor that which is evil; cleave to that which is good. Be kindly affectionate one to another with brotherly love; in honor preferring one another; Not slothful in business; fervent in spirit; serving the Lord; (Romans 12:3-11 KJV)! Lord, we shall serve in excellence in humility, clothed with the garment of a servant, waiting on you, Lord who has the power to exalt!

Move by Your spirit so that we are anointed afresh! I pray all this and give glory to You who is worthy! In Jesus' Name, Amen.

His Power My Words

Gracious Father,

As You have made us heirs of the promise, we pray Your word: But, beloved, we are persuaded better things of you, and things that accompany salvation, though we thus speak. For God is not unrighteous to forget your work and labor of love, which ye have shewed toward his name, in that ye have ministered to the saints, and do minister. And we desire that every one of you do shew the same diligence to the full assurance of hope unto the end: That ye be not slothful, but followers of them who through faith and patience inherit the promises. For when God made promise to Abraham, because he could swear by no greater, he sware by himself, Saying, Surely blessing I will bless thee, and multiplying I will multiply thee. And so, after he had patiently endured, he obtained the promise. For men verily swear by the greater: and an oath for confirmation is to them an end of all strife. (Hebrews 6:9-16 KJV).

Lord God, we keep looking up and keep our minds set on things above that are natural lives are also set in order! We live and walk by the faith You have given us and never drawing back, but feeding our spirit man more and more through prayer, fasting, studying Your word, true worship and praise! We ARE STILL HUNGRY, LORD! We do all things so that You are glorified, O Lord! Your word is truth, sure, perfect and tried! Glory to Your name, Lord! We set our affections on You and give glory, in Jesus' name, Amen!

Karen L. Northern

Father God,

We thank You for being the Everlasting God who can never lie, who can never fail who never sleeps nor slumbers! Father God, thank You for reigning supreme over every circumstance that appears to set us off our divinely purposed paths easily. Thank You for the immutability that shifts with our inconsistent ways. Thank You for being detailed, delineated, aligned and attuned to the needs of an imperfect people. Thank you, Holy Spirit, for apprehending our hearts, minds and spirits and empowering us to move past this earthly realm to chase after things that seem unattainable. We press, strive, endeavor to never miss Your move in our daily lives as You lead, guide, protect, convict, tell us the God truth about ourselves and others. We thank You for a perpetual overflow of Your glory to be shown through our service to you. We honor our heavenly seats; never relinquishing them for this lower life as our affections are for premium/holy grade living! We glorify in all we do! In Jesus' matchless name, Amen!

His Power My Words

Father,

As You have graced us once again with a new day with new mercies, we yet REJOICE IN YOU! Hallelujah! We are full of Your spiritual sap and vigor on today. Lord God, believing we are all that You say and more in Christ Jesus!

Father, we thank You that we are chosen and that You chose us to be fitly joined together with one another and an under-shepherd who hears Your voice and obeys! You placed a word in him/her so rich and Lord on today we pray Your word:

That ye may be mindful of the words which were spoken before by the holy prophets, and of the commandment of us the apostles of the Lord and Savior: Knowing this first, that there shall come in the last days scoffers, walking after their own lusts, And saying, Where is the promise of his coming? for since the fathers fell asleep, all things continue as they were from the beginning of the creation. For this, they willingly are ignorant that by the word of God the heavens were of old, and the earth standing out of the water and in the water. Whereby the world that then was being overflowed with water, perished: But the heavens and the earth, which are now, by the same word are kept in store, reserved unto fire against the day of judgment and perdition of ungodly men. But, beloved, be not ignorant of this one thing, that one day is with the Lord as a thousand years, and a thousand years as one day. The Lord is not slack concerning his promise, as some men count slackness; but is longsuffering to us-ward, not willing that any should perish, but that all should come to repentance. But the day of the Lord will come as a thief in the night; in the which the heavens shall pass away with a great noise, and the elements shall melt with fervent heat, the earth also and the works that are therein shall be burned up. Seeing then that all these things shall be dissolved, what manner of persons ought ye to be in all holy conversation and godliness? Looking for and hasting unto the coming of the day of God, wherein the heavens being on fire shall be dissolved, and the elements shall melt with fervent heat? Nevertheless we, according to his promise, look for new heavens and a new earth, wherein dwelleth righteousness. Wherefore, beloved, seeing that ye look for such things, be diligent that ye may be found of him in peace, without spot, and blameless. And account that the longsuffering of our Lord is salvation; even as our beloved brother Paul also according to the wisdom given unto him hath written unto you; Ye therefore, beloved, seeing ye know these things before, beware lest ye also, being led away with the error of the wicked, fall from Your own steadfastness. But grow in grace, and in the knowledge of our Lord and Savior Jesus Christ. To him be glory both now and forever. Amen. (2 Peter 3:2-15, 17, 18 KJV).

Lord God, I bless You for Your word and pray that we are guided by Your eyes and each step we take we walk circumspectly of Your word! I bless Your name, Lord God! Give You glory because You are THE ONE, TRUE, LIVING GOD, in Jesus' Name, Amen!

His Power My Words

Father God,

I thank You for being unchanging and consistent, our God who sees us and has graced us with a new day full of new mercies! I thank for You each family member and friend that will pray this prayer because I give thanks for them and that Your peace, joy, comfort, love and hope surrounds them daily. I thank You that they love and know you, Jesus as Savior, Wonderful Counselor, Everlasting Father and the wicked one touches them not! I come humbly as I know how, laying aside every weight and sin to thank You for others, Father: "Look not every man on his own things, but every man also on the things of others. Let this mind be in you, which was also in Christ Jesus:" Philippians 2:4-5 KJV I pray these and all things and glorify you, Father God in the matchless name of Jesus, Amen!

Karen L. Northern

My Devotions

"Beloved, if God so loved us, we ought also to love one another. No man hath seen God at any time. If we love one another, God dwelleth in us, and his love is perfected in us."
1 John 4:11-12 KJV

Loving God and others is a serious responsibility. It REQUIRES A MATURE "ATTITUDE." SPIRITUAL MATURATION OR PERFECTION OF THE HUMAN SPIRIT assists us in loving each other past our faults/human conditions; allowing us to see each other the way our Heavenly Father sees each of us. As we "grow up" in the Lord, we are able by His love to expound on and share the breadth, depth, height and length of His love. The sharing of His love is not associated with our current emotional status but rather His love that is shed abroad in our heart by the Holy Spirit (Romans 5:5b). The greatest example of love was selfless and a willing sacrifice with which we were bought and paid for by our Savior Jesus Christ!

Father God, we thank You that You loved us first and this love is progressive and mature. It spreads from You to Jesus to us to others and back again, in the name of Jesus, Amen.

#AGAPELOVE

#lovingpasttheoffenses

#humblysubmittedtooneanother

#kindlyaffectioned

"But the God of all grace, who hath called us unto his eternal glory by Christ Jesus, after that ye have suffered a while, make You perfect, stablish, strengthen, settle you." 1 Peter 5:10 KJV

BY HIS GRACE, UNMERITED FAVOR, and UNDESERVED KINDNESS are we chosen by Christ Jesus even before the foundation of this world! We attend primary, secondary school and even gain collegiate achievements. Throughout it all, we must know that God purposed every step. As we follow His prescriptive and perfect will, example of love, ministry, His sacrifice through His victorious death and resurrection shows us that NOTHING we suffer in this present day is insurmountable! WHEN WE COME OUT ON THE OTHER SIDE OF IT, MATURE IN US WHOLENESS AND NO NEED FOR ABSOLUTELY ANYTHING!

Father God, this present world can never present any trial, tribulation or trouble that You have not foreseen and surely that Your grace cannot settle to establish us in Your perfection for Your glory in Jesus' name, Amen!

#COUNTITALLJOY

#MATURITYCOSTS

"But we all, with open face beholding as in a glass the glory of the Lord, are changed into the same image from glory to glory, even as by the Spirit of the Lord." 2 Corinthians 3:18 KJV

A giving of oneself over to the Lord is a CONTINUAL process! DAILY, we must RENEW OUR COMMITMENT to the Lord through praise, prayer and worship so that He and He alone is GLORIFIED! If we stare at ourselves long enough in the mirror, something about our face becomes unfamiliar. We want an inward and outward change that only the glory of the Lord can provide. That only His sacrifice could ever have obtained. The profit gained from loss of "self" and gaining Christ is phenomenal. In gaining Him or obtaining access to the Father, the Son and Spirit play integral parts. Through this process, we are washed and renewed by the Holy Spirit and the soul (the veil) is removed! Access granted!

#committotheprocess

#Spiritsoulbodyinthatorder

Father God, we thank You that the prescriptive solution for the change required in each us is to be Spirit-filled and Spirit-led with soul and mind following in subjection to it. We submit, Holy Spirit that we experience the glory of the Lord in our lives, in Jesus' name, Amen.

"Blessed are the undefiled in the way, who walk in the law of the Lord. Blessed are they that keep his testimonies and that seek him with the whole heart." Psalms 119:1-2 KJV

We are presented with a choice between life and death; blessing and cursing. Our "YES" to the Lord must remain a yes and not waver. We do so by continuing to trust in the Lord's consistency and immutability regarding His mercy towards us. His position has not change as should our walk and commitment not change. The whole duty of man is to keep the Lord's commandments so that sin does not enter. With the help, grace and mercy of our Heavenly Father and gift of eternal life given by the sacrifice of our Lord and Savior, Jesus Christ; we can choose to LIVE TODAY and KEEP LIVING IN AND THROUGH HIM! It is not easy BUT IT IS A BLESSING!

#choosinglife

#Hisblessingsandbenefitspackagearebarnone

Father God, thank You for teaching us to run the way of Your commandments. Search us to see if there is any wicked way in us, and lead us in the way everlasting, in Jesus' name. Amen.

"But as it is written, Eye hath not seen, nor ear heard, neither have entered into the heart of man, the things which God hath prepared for them that love him. But God hath revealed them unto us by his Spirit: for the Spirit searcheth all things, yea, the deep things of God." 1 Corinthians 2:9-10 KJV

We are not prepared for what the Lord has on display for us in the Spirit because we have to be sensitive to His Spirit. Our spiritual ears and eyes must be open and in a receiving mode at all times to search what the Lord is depositing into the Spirit realm. We must also love the Lord and He must have "pole" position or first place in our hearts and minds. If this is so, our spirit-man will automatically take first place because we are in the perfect will of God. What He has prepared will show up in the natural and set this world on its ears! When you LOVE the Lord with your whole mind, soul, heart and might, there is a SPIRITUAL connection that transcends all understanding. Watch out for what is coming, it will be explosive!

#Godwillblowyourmind

#BelievetoseeHiswondrousworkstowardsyou

Father God, You are the apple of my eye, my first love and there is none beside You; I thank You as You prepare and perform Your wondrous works in the Spirit. As I believe to see them, Father, may they manifest in the realm of this earth, in Jesus' name, Amen.

"And be ye kind one to another, tenderhearted, forgiving one another, even as God for Christ's sake hath forgiven you."
Ephesians 4:32 KJV

Forgiveness is a God-given commodity that sometimes we don't readily give but always like to receive. When we are the offender, we have a million and one reason why we said what we said when we said it, or did what we did when we did it; not taking the receiver's heart into mind. OH, BUT THOSE SENSITIVE to the Spirit of the Living God and the "check" it provides to our own spirit/heart/mind remember their own faux pas/transgressions/carnalities/sin states and QUICKLY FORGIVE! LIGHTBULB, ILLUMINATION OCCURS, the show-me-to-me moment occurs! CHRIST FORGIVES/FORGAVE, so if we are to imitate or be called His followers, forgiveness should be in our repertoire of CHRISTLIKE attributes. Let our minds be also in Christ Jesus.

"Search me, O God, and know my heart: try me, and know my thoughts: And see if there is any wicked way in me, and lead me in the way everlasting." Psalms 139:23-24 KJV

Asking someone else's opinion of you is sometime a great thing to do. We don't always have the most honest opinion of ourselves. As early as primary school, we were asked to trade test papers with one another for grading purposes. We could barely concentrate on the paper we were grading because we wanted to know how many red X's were marked on our test. It didn't feel good, if we missed the mark of a passing grade. THANKS TO GOD FOR THE HOLY SPIRIT! He searches us, leads us, and shows us to us!

Father God, DAILY, I thank and praise You for searching my heart and mind to keep me in Your PERFECT WILL THAT I MAY RUN THE WAY OF YOUR COMMANDMENTS, in Jesus' name, Amen!

#HolyGhostintrospection

#youknowLordwhetherIamrightorwrong

"There is no fear in love; but perfect love casteth out fear: because fear hath torment. He that feareth is not made perfect in love." 1 John 4:18 KJV

Remember that person who made your stomach churn with anxiety EVERY time You saw them? Ah, the EMOTIONS of love! Maybe it especially caused you grief and pain when someone said they loved you and then suddenly the love was gone! Well, there are three types of love: brotherly love (philios), erotic love (eros) and unconditional (agape). Love should never cause torment or pain. Unconditionally, as the Lord has loved us with an undying love! It doesn't mean we should willfully disobey Him, but it shows the grace by which we are saved. He loved us enough to die and surrender His will for us. How much more should we?

Father God, Because Your love surrounds me like a shield, I am NEVER fearful, in Jesus' name, Amen!

#GODHASGOTME

"Hereby perceive we the love of God, because he laid down his life for us: and we ought to lay down our lives for the brethren."
1 John 3:16 KJV

How many times have you sacrificed so that someone else could benefit from it? Could you imagine accusation after being wedged against you that were untrue? Every one of them maligning your true character but you chose not to defend yourself because your silence was paramount to save humanity. Could you sacrifice yourself or your only beloved son to save a people who said they loved him, but quickly turned their backs on him and asked for death by the most brutal torture possible? Well, our God did just that for us because His love is true!

Father God, thank You that we have the GREATEST example of love in our LORD AND SAVIOR, JESUS CHRIST who WILLINGLY laid down His life for us because HE LOVES US TO LIFE, His Mighty name, Amen!

"O the depth of the riches both of the wisdom and knowledge of God! How unsearchable are his judgments, and his ways past finding out!" Romans 11:33 KJV

Have you ever spent hours upon hours studying course content for a class and still came out feeling as if you know absolutely nothing about it? Sometimes, it can be the same way when we approach the word of God as if it is course content! God's wisdom, revelation, and riches are available because it is His will to unlock them by His Spirit for our own destiny and purposes in Him. When we attempt to misuse them, then we may as well be a preschooler in an AP Chemistry class expecting to comprehend and apply the information being taught. God's will is perfect and individual for each of us and worth searching for through prayer and supplication.

Father God, thank You that Your wisdom, glory, revelation knowledge, and riches are past finding out but I'm so glad that they are AVAILABLE to those who seek Your face, in Jesus' name, Amen.

#stillinprayermode

"But the mercy of the Lord is from everlasting to everlasting upon them that fear him, and his righteousness unto our children's children;" Psalms 103:17 KJV

When the Israelites were in the wilderness, they had a cloud to lead them by day and a pillar of fire to lead them by night. When they needed sustenance (food and water) manna and quail rained down from heaven and water sprung from a rock. Their deliverance from a place of captivity and bondage was orchestrated by our GOD whose MERCY and LOVE are from EVERLASTING TO EVERLASTING and GENERATION TO GENERATION. WE SERVE A RELATIONAL GOD! Fast-forward to today where we experience war, captivity, bondage (physically, financially and psychologically), impaired physical and mental health as well as poor stewardship. Through the LIBERTY and EMANCIPATION paid for by our Savior, Christ Jesus, we are truly set at Liberty and safety! As we learn to revere our Father, His word and His doings, we HONOR what's been done and what's to come! NOW THAT'S LOVE!

Father God, we thank You that we have never been left directionless or forsaken in any area or aspect of our lives, in Jesus' name, Amen.

> "And whatsoever ye do, do it heartily, as to the Lord, and not unto men; Knowing that of the Lord ye shall receive the reward of the inheritance: for ye serve the Lord Christ."
> Colossians 3:23-24 KJV

While working at ANYTHING, a spirit of humility, compassion, and love for that which we do and those whom you serve is imperative! If we hate what we do, it will become apparent to those we serve, especially the Lord. The Lord is looking for the accuracy of our response in all we do. A little lovingkindness goes a long way! Our PASSION/LOVE for serving the Lord should be our thermostat or gauge as to how diligently we demonstrate His works through our work so He is glorified! Our heart should be toward Him in all we do so His qualities are seen in all that we do! Jesus' template for a work ethic began early. At 12, he was teaching in the synagogue, he completed his ministry in 3 years; without a home or luxuries/amenities and minus the murmuring and complaining. Working as unto the Lord pays "dividends" too immeasurable to number!

Father God, thank You for the blueprint for work ethics set by our Lord and Savior Jesus Christ as well as other forerunners who await the guaranteed promise of eternal life, in Jesus' name, Amen.

> "Humble yourselves therefore under the mighty hand of God, that he may exalt you in due time:"
> 1 Peter 5:6 KJV

We work a job for a number of years and we expect that if we do a good job, a promotion should be ours. We expect accolades, promotion and applause because we worked for it! It doesn't always pan out that way! Eventually, after saving and giving into a pension system or working at our business, we retire. For some, the retirement place is the very same place from which they began. I found the key to promotion is HUMILITY AND GODLY CONFIDENCE! I place my confidence and trust in the One who made me humble myself before Him. He orders my steps in my natural and spiritual life so that any promotion is by HIS HAND and IRREVOCABLE!

#Godsmeritsystemisthegreatest

#Stayhumble

#Godsopendoorscanneverbeshut

Father God, thank You for keeping us in the seasons of waiting in humility for Your exaltation, because when it occurs, none can reverse it but You. In Jesus' name, Amen!

"There hath no temptation taken you but such as is common to man: but God is faithful, who will not suffer you to be tempted above that ye are able; but will with the temptation also make a way to escape, that ye may be able to bear it."
1 Corinthians 10:13 KJV

There is a way out accompanying every wind of adversity, trial, difficulty or temptation. However, you must also have an innate desire to escape it. If the temptation is repeated, it is difficult to find the exit. The Holy Spirit CONTINUALLY contends with the temptation to cause you to recognize it as it really is! Then He prepares a way of escape that we either take or ignore. The prompting of the Holy Spirit is a gentleman and He is not pushy like the tempter, who comes to bring the detour or temptation. We must be vigilant and sober-minded when presented with "suspect" choices. The way of escape is usually nearby.

Father God, I thank You that No matter what I'm facing, if I follow the leading of the Holy Spirit and Your word, You are JUST AND FAITHFUL to bring me through it! It may not BE MY WAY, but if I trust Him I'm sure to come out of the process/test/trial/temptation more mature, whole, and in need of absolutely NOTHING, in Jesus' name, Amen!

#HisgraceisTRULYSUFFICIENT

#overcomingtemptationsareonestogrowon

#IamTRULYbehindinnogoodthing

Karen L. Northern

"For the Lord taketh pleasure in his people: he will beautify the meek with salvation." Psalms 149:4 KJV

Our Heavenly Father planned for each of us and chose us before the foundation of this world! We are a MARVELOUS WORK IN HIS SIGHT! We are not now nor will we ever be an afterthought! He wishes that NONE would perish! God is mindful of EACH AND EVERY PERSON, but salvation is contingent upon our response to the invitation to serve Him that is extended by our Lord and Savior Jesus Christ! SERVICE TO OUR GOD TAKES THE SAME HUMILITY, DISCIPLINE, PLEASUREAND COMMITMENT IT TOOK TO CREATE US!

#weareHisgoodpleasureandworkmanship

Father God, I thank You that You take pleasure in saving Your people, in Jesus' name, Amen!

"Before destruction the heart of man is haughty, and before honor is humility." Proverbs 18:12 KJV

There is a rap lyric that says, "check yourself before you wreck yourself". WOOOOOW! If we dig into that, we can find the wisdom needed to know that humility is paramount in our daily lives and should be a driving force in our relationships. Look before you leap, be slow to speak, quick to hear/apologize and/or try to understand another's (or better yet) your own motives before moving forward! Destruction or progression are the two options—choose wisely.

#itisamatteroftheheart

#guarditwithALLdiligence

#lettheHolySpiritdrive

Father God, we bless You that humility is honorable, in Jesus' name, Amen!

"If we confess our sins, he is faithful and just to forgive us our sins, and to cleanse us from all unrighteousness."
1 John 1:9 KJV

It never feels good when someone points out Your deficits or deficiencies. At one time in school, we were allowed to correct tests, quizzes, makes assessments of one another and the like. This took trust and patience on the part of the teacher. He/She could also trust the fidelity of each student and allow self-assessment. We must trust the Lord enough to know He sees ALL we do and is there when we do it. If we confess it, turn from it and never turn back, He will forgive! He is faithful! In a day when ANYTHING and EVERYTHING goes according to man, I still choose to stand with God and ask Him to SHOW ME TO ME every day. Show me how I err and fall short before I can speak to anyone or anything else. I must have a clean bill of "SPIRITUAL HEALTH" to move forward in my day!

#holinessstartsathome

Father God, I trust You implicitly to be faithful to forgive as I confess my sins of omission and commission never to turn back, in the name of Jesus, Amen!

"For I reckon that the sufferings of this present time are not worthy to be compared with the glory which shall be revealed in us." Romans 8:18 KJV

Every time I open my mouth to complain about physical and emotional pain, trials, troubles and the struggles of everyday life, my SENSITIVITY to the leading of Spirit of God overrides THEM ALL! I begin to THINK ON the FACT that I was PURCHASED WITH A HIGH PRICE BY MY SAVIOR and it shifts me into a different mindset. I can't help BUT TO SHOUT PRAISES and KNOW that my REWARD IS NEAR!

#mustwatchovermymind&heart

#thislightafflictionisgoingtopayoffifIdonotfaint

Father God, thank You for a mind to praise and not complain because nothing I'm suffering can compare to the glory that awaits me if I continue pressing until the end, in Jesus' name, Amen!

Karen L. Northern

"But seek ye first the kingdom of God, and his righteousness; and all these things shall be added unto you."
Matthew 6:33 KJV

In a Get-It-Quick Society seeking the Lord first is a dual duty. My thoughts and intents are continuously geared toward the mind of Christ and the very center of His will. Secondly, my deeds must reflect His will through submission to it, obedience and right living. The more mature I become in Him, the more I realize and recognize that through seeking Him; my needs are continually met and I am complete and lacking NOTHING!

Father God, thank You for meeting every need by riches which encompass every aspect of my life including finances so that I am a servant as well as kingdom contributor who is never in need of any good or beneficial thing, in Jesus' name, Amen.

"For I know the thoughts that I think toward you, saith the Lord, thoughts of peace, and not of evil, to give You an expected end. Then shall ye call upon me, and ye shall go and pray unto me, and I will hearken unto you. And ye shall seek me, and find me, when ye shall search for me with all Your heart."
Jeremiah 29:11-13 KJV

The DIFFERENCE between how we view the enemy's threats to kill, steal and destroy versus the Lord's TESTED AND BLESSED ASSURANCES, ARE A MATTER OF OUR FAITH! The LORD IS INTIMATELY IN THE DETAILS, not the devil! We are in COVENANT with the Lord, not the devil! As we prayfully seek our Father, the enemy's intrusion into the details can only be thwarted/cast down. This is especially true, when we are ASSURED of what we know, think, and say about our relationship with the Lord! THE EXPECTED END IS BLESSED, ACCORDING TO OUR FAITH! Even the captivity setup by our own disobedience will prompt the Lord to act on our behalf.

#letitbesountoyou

#ourendshallbeGREATER

"If my people, which are called by my name, shall humble themselves, and pray, and seek my face, and turn from their wicked ways; then will I hear from heaven, and will forgive their sin, and will heal their land. Now mine eyes shall be open, and mine ears attent unto the prayer that is made in this place."
2 Chronicles 7:14-15 KJV

A place of surrender in the Lord should continually originate from seeking the Lord relationally to obtain guidance for our individual, corporate and spiritual lives. In the wait, our God honors His servants who come with sincerity, humbled, open with penitent hearts towards Him, and laying their requests at His feet so healing and forgiveness can occur!

Father God, You are amazingly consistent yet flexible for my needs to keep in the center of Your will and for that, I say thank you in Jesus' name, Amen!

www.ingramcontent.com/pod-product-compliance
Lightning Source LLC
Chambersburg PA
CBHW051710090426
42736CB00013B/2624